WHERE WE'RE GOING, WHERE WE'VE BEEN

☙❧

Arnold Johnston

FUTURECYCLE PRESS
www.futurecycle.org

Cover design and artwork by Linda Rzoska; author photo by Sarah Matyczyn; interior book design by Diane Kistner; Stempel Garamond LT Pro text and titling

Library of Congress Control Number: 2019949715

Copyright © 2020 Arnold Johnston
All Rights Reserved

Published by FutureCycle Press
Athens, Georgia, USA

ISBN 978-1-942371-83-0

For Debby, always

CONTENTS

Syzygy in Center Field..7
Spectators As We Are..9
The Poet Visits Lake Michigan...13
A Sort of Sestina..14
Contract Language..16
Reduction...17
Moon Goddess...18
Canzone: The Tree in Our Bed..20
Double Sonnet: Sunday Drive...23
Old Debts..24
Sestina: His Own Bright Music (1952)..26
What The Earth Taught Us...28
What's Underneath...30
Dance Russe *Revisited: For William Carlos Williams*...................32
These Lovers: Amor Vincit Omnia...33
Rondeau: Ocean in the Shell...34
Pantoum: Where We're Going, Where We've Been......................35
Sestina: Libbie Remembers..36
Sonnet for Carol..38
The Poet Does Yardwork...39
The Poet Considers His Plant..40
The Poet Takes a Good Look at Himself.....................................41
The Consultant's Advice to the Candidate..................................42
Pusillanimous Poem..43
The Poet Has a Midlife Crisis..44
The Poet Calls It a Day..45
Spoiled Baby...46
Bookworm, a Fragment...48
Revelation...49
Alchemy: A Sestina...50
The Great Reviser..52
Pantoum: Then to Now...54
The Poet Celebrates Scots' New Year Seven P.M., EST................55
Radioactive...56
Pantoum: The Damned Can Tell Us...57
United States of Discord..58

Something to Work With *59*
Losing What Seems Most Dear *60*
Sooner Than Later *61*
Rainbow *62*
Measuring Grace *63*
Holes That Can't Be Patched *64*
Sparrows *65*
Romeo and Juliet, from the Balcony *66*
The Poet Contemplates a Shrine *67*
Deborah, Always *68*

SYZYGY IN CENTER FIELD

syzygy: 1. in astronomy, either of two opposing points in the orbit of a heavenly body. 2. in ancient prosody, a group of two feet, as a dipody

"We will be called The Syzygies"
—Norman Kurilik, softball manager

We can't lose this one.
I believe that, standing here in center field,
Watching Tony suck up grounders,
Gun the ball to Norm at first,
Bill pounding down the line from third
Under a soft foul fly,
Rob pivoting from second for the quick d.p.
Every now and then Jeff fungoes one
And I move, easy, under the high arc,
Another can of corn.
Or Stu pinwheels after a liner,
Snags it, waves his glove,
An ice-cream cone.
The fat guy's catcalls from the bleachers—
What does he know?

But the games came and went.
Sudden grounders skimmed across the field,
Caromed off legs and forearms;
Our pegs bounced in to second or to third.
Long flies and bloopers dropped among us,
Heavy as stones. Home plate acquired,
From passing feet, a layer of dust
No ump could ever brush away.
I watched it all from center field,
Then right, that grave for guys the manager
Wants buried, and finally behind the plate,
Squatting like a backstop Buddha,
Meditating on those last indignities:
The coach's box; the bench.

Most of us are gone now:
Tony to a different hot dog stand,
Bill to Wichita and dreams of Nashville,
Stu to slide those bad knees under a typewriter.
Only Jeff's still out there, cracking the long ones,
And Norm, still searching in his bones
For Sparky Anderson and Pee Wee Reese.
Now I run in place, do sit-ups, dumbbell curls,
Still in shape, but off the basepaths.
Like the fat guy in the bleachers
I begin to forget what a bat feels like,
And to learn what he knew all along:
We can't win this one.

SPECTATORS AS WE ARE

Sleet patters across my car's window
In the South Beach parking lot. Sitting
Here, hand in hand, we lament spring's slow
Sweep up the coastline from Chicago.

You're not sure I want to be with you;
You know I'm capable of running,
And you're angry. You point out how few
Years we may have, and I can't argue.

You press on: "We should think of each day
As the last gift we'll get." I'm nodding,
But I know we seldom find a way
To live our lives like that. And I say,

"We're never ready for disaster."
For even when we know what's coming,
Foreknowledge never helps us master
Our fate. Like the poor drunk bastard

At the local winefest; the bozo
Thought he'd end the night's fun by walking
Around the city parking ramp's low
Parapet. Falling, he said, "Oh, no."

Could it be he really didn't know,
Despite his friends' and his wife's pleading,
That he might plunge sixty feet onto
The dark pavement down there? And if so,

Can his brief fall convince us that we,
Ourselves, when life finds us performing
Our own crazy stunts, will probably
Feel the same thrill of surprise to be

Dying, too? How can it slip our minds,
Or can a part of us be lying,
That we forget how frail a tie binds
Us to the real world? What is it blinds

Us at such moments? Perhaps the sense
That we're immortal, or just watching
Our own lives, as if experience
Might be a TV show, more intense,

Perhaps, but no more real. Remember
The man who was videotaping
Skydivers, and who, as their 'chutes were
Blossoming below in the cold air,

Stepped out to join them? What the tape shows
Is the cameraman's realizing
That he has no 'chute. We know he knows
When he looks down and the picture goes

Crazy. As long as nothing is real
The camera's focused, recording
Everything; but when he starts to feel
For his ripcord and his veins congeal,

He spurns vision like a false lover.
And now we sit together, watching
Lake Michigan from the dry cover
Of my Toyota. Seagulls hover

Above the waves that attack the dock,
Neither birds nor gray water caring
About us or each other. We talk
Of all this, and of people who walk

Out on the pier to see the lake's show
Of power, despite weather warnings

And common sense. Now and then, we know,
Someone's swept away and sucked below,

Battered by the waves, and drowned. And I
Wonder if, when they find they're breathing
Water and know they're about to die,
They spend a moment wondering why

Their lives seemed like something they had paid
To watch, all the moments unfolding
Like someone else's story. "They made
The choices," you say. "They could have stayed

Where they were safe and warm. Whatever
They believed, life wasn't happening
To them. We make it happen. Never
Forget that. You can be too clever

On the subject, brood too much over
Whys and wherefores, and avoid choosing
Your own turning points: wife or lover,
Here or there. You know you can't cover

All the bets. You can't have certainty;
It's all a risk. There's no real knowing
Till you try. Some risks are bad, but we
Aren't one of them. So there." That's me

All over, as you know, spectator
And recorder, but seldom acting
For myself, habitual waiter
On eventual turns of fate or

Chance. So I'm the one I'm speaking of,
Who thinks life can be lived by waiting
For someone else to decide when love
Is over. My doubt goes hand in glove

With your certainty. And yet we lay
This morning on the beach, sheltering
Behind a low dune, watching the way
Snow formed brief stars on your coat. You'd say

It's the best image I could have drawn.
With that thought, I start the car. Nearing
The road, we glance back at the lake. One
Gull hangs there. You smile. And I drive on.

THE POET VISITS LAKE MICHIGAN

Hunkered, he's here beside her, picking stones
Along the wind-chopped margin of this lake
They've found their way to, where they've come to rake
Through memories like ash or blackened bones.
A lone fly bats his temples, backs off, drones
Away. He looks up, sees the lighthouse bake
Under the late summer sun. Will this make
A difference? Will it modulate their tones?
Or will they file away this weekend, chalk
Another try off the list as they edge
Their way to nothing? "Is it going to rain?"
She asks. Now they've come down to such small talk;
They shore up these civilities, a hedge
Against inflated hope, to keep them sane.

A SORT OF SESTINA

Across from me a pretty waitress tops
Up the coffee mug the hippie Jesus
Holds; she smiles, red-lipped, like you.
He smokes Camels, wears a watch cap; his old
Quilted jacket reminds me of a life
Put by, an era almost lost, indistinct,

When you and I were more like him, you
Whose sickness trails my thoughts, indistinct
But always there. I look at the old
Photos of this town, and at the tops
Of sconces — nothing of you or Jesus
There, where red and green elves cling for dear life

Amid garlands of gold tinsel, old
Stories lost within older. New life
Transformed by miracle into Jesus:
The process for me is indistinct,
But at last no stranger than what you
Hold within your body. If the tops

Of milk dispensers can grow indistinct
With Christmas trees, perhaps all the old
Tales are true; if they can kill the life
That grows malign within you,
Perhaps I'll spin French's mustard pots like tops
Across these tables, jogging Jesus

From his Coke and Camels into life
Again. If they can cure you,
I'll pound formica tabletops,
Make cream containers jump for Jesus,
With everything before me indistinct,
Blurred by the hope that we'll grow old

Together. And now I see Jesus
Rise. Our eyes meet over the tops
Of heads; then I hear his voice, indistinct,
Bidding the waitress farewell. And life
Resumes its fold and coil. But those old
Patterns won't displace my thoughts of you

And Christmas, if Jesus, indistinct
Though His life may be to you
And me, tops His own miracle, as in days of old.

CONTRACT LANGUAGE

What price that woman's touch?
Anything within reason.
No. That's not the range we had in mind.

Outside, winter settles on the library,
The angled concrete paths; it clears the air,
Squeezes warmth out of standing water,
Freezes locks open, or shut, regardless.
You think of all the small deaths you've died;
They've taught you nothing of finality.
You know the value of a skid, how to
Steer into a dollar, why life imitates
Bodies, where some of the art is buried.
But you can't say why she, particular,
Discrete, catches in your mind like the end
Of breathing, why your knuckles, the hair
On the back of your hand, resurrect
The plane of her cheek, now, as you watch
Winter emptying the day.

You'd rip twenties into green snowflakes,
Fishtail and spin your way across Nebraska,
Dig up murdered legions and confess,
Hack continuously at time
With pen, brush, chisel, laser beam,
For that face, now, for that small death.

What's outside reason? My honor? My hope?
Now you're talking. We can do business.
Sign here.

REDUCTION

> "As a writer, one of your most important duties is to search your
> dictionary for words appropriate to your message and audience"
> —Kirkland & Dilworth, *Concise English Handbook*

You've brought me to a certain state,
Condition, arrangement, as to reduce
Glass to powder, or a person, perhaps,
To desperation, brought under control
Or authority. I'm an expression
Simplified; you've done it elegantly,
Adjusting by making allowances.
You've thinned the mixture by adding spirits.
In the process I've become less rusty,
Purer, closer to my elemental
State. When I'm with you, I'm simpler, my life
Less complex, too, as if something has slipped
Into place, restored, like a fractured bone.
And I, in turn, lessen your negatives
In density by slow development,
Maturing us into the haploid state,
Our own meiotic simplification,
Before we're both reduced at last, in life's
Good time, to our own absurd conclusion,
That proposition no one can refute.

MOON GODDESS

She circles me, keeping her distance,
Knowing I'm under her influence, a little crazy.
My tides rise to her changeable aspects;
Her distant calm fazes me constantly.
Her face, the one she always shows,
Wears its beauty well; I never tire
Of that complex topography. But I want more:
I want to see her other side, the one
Our separate motions cause to be averted,
That puzzle only darkness can solve.
Her gravity is less than mine. And why not?
I'm heavier, take myself too seriously.
She thinks I see mystery where none exists.
She has forgotten, or ignores, the history
Or fantasy that draws us to each other,
The pull I feel inside, convincing me
That something tore her from me once,
Long before memory, and left an ocean
In her place, a deep familiar puzzle.
She seems content with larger laws—
What I can't live with, or without—
Knows the balance that holds bodies in place,
Foresees tsunamis, earthquakes, fumaroles,
All the lunatic foul weather of disturbed inertia,
Even the final plunge to where we both belong:
Together. The puzzle complete.
Explosion. Fireworks. Chaos. Oblivion.

    Luna. The Earth. I flatter myself,
Exaggerate your beauty: it's too much.
We are ourselves, human, small.
No stars will tumble if our orbits merge.
And even should gravity prevail, if earth and moon
On some unlikely day fell free together,

We'd be among the millions blown sky-high,
No special fanfare, no soaring choir:
Little creatures here and gone.
But if it happens, as the last earthly
Fragments fly, I hope we're there together,
Declaring one our own, and celebrating,
In some old way, our new moon.

CANZONE: THE TREE IN OUR BED

When we planned our new bedroom, a tree
Held prior claim. Eighty feet from the earth,
Its upper branches laced against the sky, that tree
Stood where our bed now stands: a cherry tree,
Double-trunked, as much acquainted with the air
As with the dirt around its roots, each tree's
Tangled footing. Long before our house, the tree
Grew here, in Fletcher Park, on this water-
Shed's mild ridge, sucking water
Through the busy topsoil, sand, and clay, a tree
Twinned from its single heart, drawn to the sun's fire
Driven from below by its own fire.

Now when I look up where leaves once fluttered, fire
From the sun is all that's left: the tree
Is gone. John and I began the job, my fear
Of heights keeping me on the ground while, far
Above, he chainsawed limbs and lowered them to earth
On sinewy nylon cord. I'd untie them, fire
Up my own saw, cut and stack the logs for fire-
Wood. Up there, he seemed a creature of air,
At home among those disappearing branches. His air
Of nonchalance set my face on fire,
As I thought how my heart would pump water
If I were in his place, and my eyes would water

In the sky's thin glare. My eyes did water,
Anyway, tears washing the fire
Of sawdust from under my eyelids. And water
Tasted good that warm May afternoon; water
Alone seemed pure enough for drinking to that tree's
Final days. I spilled the last drops of water
On crabgrass and peonies. Above me, John drank no
    water;

Busy and agile, he brought that old tree to earth.
It was yours and mine, but with more claim to the earth
Than our own. We're impermanent, water-
Logged, our trunks filled out with bags of air,
While that survivor lived through lightning, rain, all
   the air's

        Truculence, until we came here. The air
Was still the next day, no hint of water
In the sky. The tree, dismantled from the high air,
Lay in pieces, stacked and piled around us. Air
Filled the space where the trunk had stood. Fired
By that success, we ringed the great stump, airy
And confident: John, Don, Virgil, Charlie, and I,
   hare-
Brained enough to think we'd move it. The tree,
Reduced to its wooden heart, clung tree-
Solid to the deep clay. And soon the air
Filled with grunts and curses as we fought the earth
With axes, saws, spades, and human will to break
   earth's

Grip on that last, obstinate mass. The earth
Won, as it will, sooner or later. No air
Of confidence marked us at the end, though earth
Gave way to machine: Virgil, with a backhoe, small
   earth-
Mover, mounted on a Bobcat, its water-
Cooled engine growling, tore the stump's roots from the
   earth,
And dug it under in the clay, dragging earth
Over that scarred place. Then he stilled the engine's
   fire
To a dying cough. Our cheers took fire
As if we'd won something, and not the earth.

We moved the cut logs, then, remnants of the tree;
We poured the concrete footings and the slab on the
 tree's

Grave. But even now, years later, I know that tree
Rises through our bed, thrusting out of the earth
Like the memory of a severed limb, high into the air,
Its spirit, like ours, still intimate with water,
Rising, as we do, over and over, to the sun's fire.

DOUBLE SONNET: SUNDAY DRIVE

On this late winter Sunday, on careful
Country roads, life slides by at forty-five.
Cold sunlight plates the hills gold as we drive
Past farmhouses in what feels like prayerful
Silence. Animals stand at rest where full
Troughs have called them. They scarcely look alive
In their calm indifference to us, who strive
So to keep moving. They stand immobile:

Spotted ponies, wool-thickened sheep, and great
Slow sows. Light stretches so taut and static
On the earth's curve, the road can't help but warp
Space and time by its motion, and we gawp
As through a boat's glass bottom, frenetic,
Alien to the quiet land's slow heartbeat.

Our transience must loosen shingles, scrape paint
From each farm we pass. The rawboned trees shake
Their wild hair. Spinster-like, they seem to ache
With condescension and mutter their faint
Curse: they've seen it all before, and it ain't
So much, the living, the dying, the break
Of too many dawns, sudden cars that take
Pale, watching faces through this stillness, saint

And sinner. We look envious, they know,
And a bit tired, headed for a bad end,
No doubt, and driving faster than we should.
They know the signs and portents don't look good
And favor no one, neutral, foe, or friend:
Each spinster lives to say, "I told you so."

OLD DEBTS

The sky freshens; light blows through the clouds.
I feel my face soften in the damp wind.
The ocean shifts, poised between gray and green.
And I say nothing.
        Waiting is my game:
Somewhere on this same water, years ago,
I stood fixed in the great vibrating bell
Of sound that fell, heavy, out of the first
Queen's foghorn. I hadn't asked to be there,
Blown along her deck one night
Like a drunken sailor, hanging
In the rush of air like ill-pinned laundry.
Did I learn then to lose myself,
Waiting for the wind's turn,
Or was it later?

        You shudder,
Hug yourself against the breeze.
You see I'm easily distracted
And find that reason for mistrust.
You wonder what I'm thinking, or of whom.

Sand stings our ankles like minute insects
Or returning blood. I begin to know
Why distances have always seemed most real
To me, why I relish long drives
Across empty spaces.

        I smile at you
And touch your arm. You brush against me,
Move away, a warm tangent;
It's not what you want.

    I squat
And pry a sand flea, all quick legs,
From the wet swirl at the sea's lace edge.
I hold it up to you. You laugh
For a while as it tickles your palm,
Then drop it, let it furrow back
Beneath the liquid shore.

    I practice
Giving, make the gesture often,
But it's never what you want. We both know
All my gifts are thoughtful, and we wait:
For the right wind,
For the quick heart's surprise.

SESTINA: HIS OWN BRIGHT MUSIC (1952)

The boy stands in his aunt's bathroom. Music
Floats on hot air from the basement, the dance
Of molecules, the puzzle of physics,
Beyond him yet, like the stirring of sex.
Oh, he eyes shapely women, but he wants
Something more childish now: he wants to mix

Mysteries, like an alchemist, to mix
From bottles and jars something like music
Out of makeup and medicine. He wants
To know why things work. Downstairs at the dance
His relatives (pinups on the wall, sex)
Swing Sammy Kaye by their highballs, physiques

Formed by tuna casseroles, the physics
Of heredity, ginger ale their mix,
Cigarette smoke filling their lungs with sex.
The boy blinks at the mirror. The music
Hangs in his head like the crystalline dance
Of colored vials behind the glass. He wants

To open them all, to make what he wants
From what's inside, to take the cheap physics
And cosmetics, conjoin them, make them dance
To a tune he hasn't thought of yet, mix
And stir their inert compounds to music.
He senses it may be better than sex,

But can't be sure; for all he knows of sex
Hangs on his aunt's wall, Vargas girls he wants
To sit and think about with no music
Or relatives around him, when physics
Will reduce to simple curves, and the mix
Of bodies means something more than a dance.

He thinks of the Hawaiian war dance,
His cousin's party-piece, and finds no sex
There, only the sullen chant with its mix
Of glottal stops and vowels. But he wants
To know why his cousin's smile, and physics,
And his urge to mix things, and the music

All seem like a dance that everyone wants
To learn. And whether it's sex or physics,
He begins to mix his own bright music.

WHAT THE EARTH TAUGHT US

An hour or so south, you told me, we could find
Sharks' teeth within the Mesozoic sludge
Dredged out along the banks of the canal.
These days, you hunt through stones and sediment,
Clip news from Olduvai; I try to write.
But I know the game: though paper may envelop
Rock, scissors will have their way.
And now a freighter slides by like a small
(Norwegian) town as we lie here and read
The ground, prostrate, nearsighted penitents,
Cautious students of our own earth; close study,
As you tell me, the only way to see.
Myopic, we note small things: slate wafers,
Crumbs of burnt cork, brittle slivers of old wood,
Glass shards. Red ants and jumping spiders move
Among islands of stubble in the sand.
Your body lies near me under a sky
That hurts to look at. We focus on the ground.

I lost my Scripto ballpoint days ago
And haven't written since. What can I hope
To find here, if I'm so blind at home?
Keep looking, you say, smiling, levered
On your elbows, sand grains in the hollow
Of your neck.

    But my ears are keen: I hear
Your husband's pen scratch legal pads eighty
Miles north.

    I find a tooth: smooth, gray-white,
Nearly perfect; sharp-edged, of course. No need
To ask if this is shark, that nagging ache
In the world's dim memory.

                You find a tooth.
I think of their tearing bloody clouds
And hunks from swimmers less well-versed, who left
No descendants to sniff for flesh in
Coastal shallows. Extinct: what sharks aren't,
Whose fossil teeth look newer than my own.

We find a necklaceful among the sand
And small debris. You always knew we would.
At every dredging site, you tell me,
New searchers for the past appear. They know
You can't dig that deep without finding something.
And you look at me:

        the day breathes out.
Neighbor. Friend. Woman.

            And I nod. You're right.
I feel us gliding in the shallows,
Notice that your smile is new, and pocket
My shark's tooth, hard fragment of this day,
Wrapped hopefully in paper against
Its dredged-up, ancient, sharp insistence.

WHAT'S UNDERNEATH

After untitled twig-and-fired-ceramic piece by Maria Scott

Frail bars, sunk deep in stone tempered by fire
That could reduce a wooden grid to ash,
Leaving just the bedrock. We never tire
Of raising cages, walls; we twine and lash

Our rickety contrivings, groove and rout,
Knowing the earth we build on will endure.
What we create to hold life in or out
Will fall, will fail, of that we may be sure,

Consumed at length by fire, flood, decay,
Or fresh mischief: for they'll huff and they'll puff
And they'll blow the house down. There is no way
To keep the wolf from the door, not enough

Of straw, sticks, bricks that we can hope to shore
Against time's ruin. Thus, Grandma prepares
To face the fiend in sheep's disguise before
Red Riding Hood—known, too, by what she wears—

Brings her woodsman, flesh or tin, to spill blood,
Felling Grandma's bane. And how can we say
What grew within the wolf, from seed to bud
To flower, will not rise up in us someday?

We need diversion and we look elsewhere,
To Munchkins, flying monkeys, talking trees,
Tornadoes whirling us from here to there,
Beyond the rainbow to our destinies.

But when we've danced through, over, or around
Each hindrance to the Emerald City's gate,
What lurks behind the light and smoke and sound?
Our mortal self, our sad and comic fate,

Pretentious oracle revealing all
Despite congenital dishonesty,
Showing the truth of our fortunate fall—
We own the power of choice that makes us free—

Showing us, too, there is no place like home.
The archetypal shrink, guiding us back
To what lies hidden near the beaten track:
The earthen bed, the pillow made of stone.

DANCE RUSSE *REVISITED:*
FOR WILLIAM CARLOS WILLIAMS

This old man's capering before a glass,
Unruly member flopping like a trout
Against his thighs and belly, puts me out
Of humor; the white half-moons of his ass
Aquiver, and the jut of his bald paunch,
Do these add up to poetry? What dumb
Dithyramb pipes him on? What nymph rose from
Memory, wreathed in his arms' circle, to launch
This gavotte in the pale light of his eyes?

Lost youth can't be what he's bouncing after:
He surely knows that's an unlikely prize.
He sees his reflection, must realize
His blunt-toed jig gives more cause for laughter
Than applause; yet dance this old gaffer does,
Stripped to his less-than-perfect form, unversed
In this muse's symmetries, a rare burst
Of life to the furnace's tuneless buzz,
Stirring his own left-footed complement.

The image glazes, slides back to the page:
I want to laugh, yet there's an element—
What?—a waxy whiff of the cerement
To come, perhaps? Still, he defies his age
And prances, scrotum swinging, in the cool
Morning, comic and tragic in each beat,
Content with the sprung rhythm of his feet.
I close the book, admit I'd be a fool
To vex a happy genius at his glass.

THESE LOVERS: AMOR VINCIT OMNIA

They make us laugh; we see ourselves entangled
In their lifelines, analyze their brief
Collisions, feel with them the way to secret doors.
We celebrate their transformations, share
Their innocence, their faith in accident;
Their simple pleasure in their victories is ours.

They plan their assignations childishly,
Meet in places where their friends will see them;
Startled, they tumble breadsticks, spill red wine,
Duck their heads, two hunchbacks on a blind date,
Drawing all eyes to where their linked hands lie
Among the crumbs and stains. Everyone knows.

They weigh their options, all heavier than air,
Cite precedents, prepare their brief for love,
Brood for days on missed phone calls, their own obliquity,
Lie sleepless, anxious and absurdly proud,
Drop hints to wives or husbands, hoping
Someone will write an ending, find a cure.

They kill themselves or those they love; they tear
Their eyes out in despair and serve them
Sunny-side up to puzzled children robed
Like judges; leave shrill testaments to lust
Or vengeance and the blood's strong will; embrace
Their sin, distracted, as they lost their hearts.

They hold each other, cry like animals;
Their bodies' friction warms what need defines,
Makes ends remote and thought remoter still.
They, too, would watch in condescension,
But they're lost, as we might hope to be
If we allow our skin to dream their dreams.

The play goes on in all its acts and forms:
These lovers: their question: "Don't we beat all?"

RONDEAU: OCEAN IN THE SHELL

Your silence is a secret you keep,
Though all of us may think we know it.
You'd rather contrive to have us sit
On your left than violate that deep
Quiet inside your skull with a cheap

Hearing aid. You've never cared a bit
That all of us may think we know it:
Your silence is a secret you keep.

I don't know if you can hear a peep
Through your right ear, but in talk your wit
Loses its nerve. At best, now, you fit
In. Every night, though, you take to sleep
Your silence; it's the secret you keep.

PANTOUM: WHERE WE'RE GOING, WHERE WE'VE BEEN

"Ed Fredkin thinks the universe is a computer"
—Robert Wright, *Three Scientists and Their Gods*

algorithm: any mechanical or recursive computational procedure.

Somewhere in the center of creation
An algorithm generates the cosmos,
And everything is information.
Spitting binary noughts and jackstraws,

An algorithm generates the cosmos.
Matter and energy change and dance,
Spitting binary noughts and jackstraws
In the ticktock of fate and chance.

Matter and energy change and dance,
Each particle and parcel's destiny
In the ticktock of fate and chance
Determined by one cosmic inquiry.

Each particle and parcel's destiny—
Mouse or quark or angel's fall—
Determined by one cosmic inquiry
At the center of it all.

Mouse or quark or angel's fall,
The best physics is metaphysics:
At the center of it all
Does an old god teach us new tricks?

The best physics is metaphysics,
And everything is information.
Does an old god teach us new tricks
Somewhere at the center of creation?

SESTINA: LIBBIE REMEMBERS

> "Come on. Big village. Be quick. Bring packs."
> —George Armstrong Custer, note
> to Captain Benteen, June 25, 1876

On the cool May morning when they rode off, a crystallized
Scrim of ground fog rose high above them; that domain
Of portents, the sky, cheated gravity,
Made a phantom troop appear where falcons
Usually wheel. Libbie recalls a wealth
Of such details, down to each eyelash

On the blaze-faced sorrel, Vic, in that eyelash-
Flicker when she touched her husband's thigh one
    last time, a moment crystallized
Forever, that no power, no wealth
Can take from the domain
Of her memory. Now, when she sees a falcon
Allowing the air to carry it above gravity,

She returns, alone, to the gravity
Of that day, that refracted vision, and soaks
    each eyelash
With a lens of tears. She remembers when George,
    her falcon,
Hung in a balloon's gondola above Confederate
    lines, watching through the crystal eyes
Of field glasses the rebels below. Their domain,
Too, lives only in memory, their wealth

Of breath spent in a lost cause. What can wealth
Buy? Not one image equal to the gravity
Of what George must have seen at Little Big Horn,
    that hostile domain.

Nothing emerges sure when memory's eyelash
Of uncertainty provides all we know: crystallized
In paint, in print, imagination makes a falcon's

Swoop of each sparrow's fall, a falcon's
Gold pinion of the coward's white feather. But
   the commonwealth
Of death speaks only of results, not causes; and
   Christ allies
Himself with those who believe, prepares the
   wealth
Of Heaven for the poor and meek. Yet an eyelash
Of faith may prevail, she knows, in the domain

History grants her man, fool or hero, a domain
Governed by reckless chance. What falcon,
She thinks, will not fall before sparrows? And
   that eyelash
Sustains her like inherited wealth,
Allows her to ignore the gravity
Of all but her hero's fate. And crystallized

In the air's domain, beyond the gross wealth
Of nations, or the falcon's stoop, or gravity,
His troop's legend floats, slighter than an
   eyelash seen through crystal eyes.

SONNET FOR CAROL

Here, where a dripping IV bag marks time,
In this town over which the big jets' flight
Paths merge to find O'Hare, anyone might
Leave her and, for the price of two thin dimes,
Call warmth and freedom. But we stand here, mime
Concern above her bed, stand through the night,
Alert for change, alive to any slight
Hitch in her breathing. TVs drone through prime
Time across the hall, next door. News can mean
Only one thing to us who wait. Raw wind
Shivers the panes, reminds us we must throw
Her ashes on the big lake. We might scream
For justice, ask to know what was her sin;
But all we find is strength to let her go.

THE POET DOES YARDWORK

The autumn air turns acrid with blue smoke
As flames take leaf and drifts of birds take flight.
He notes she's leaning on her rake, a sight
Inevitable as the years. The choke-
Cherry trees loose pits like buckshot. The cloak
Of green that shades the yard is gone; the bite
Of the north wind waits. He bags leaves, contrite,
A penitent who tried to shed the yoke
Of domesticity, the dominion
Of wedlock and good sense. Most nights he lies
Beside her now and listens to the clink
Of wind chimes from the eaves; their opinion
Seems at such times the only truth. He sighs,
And turns to dream as some men turn to drink.

THE POET CONSIDERS HIS PLANT

His poinsettia straggles her green leader
From his TV stand's top shelf. No zealous
Gardener, he's never built a trellis
For any vine, and in the theater
Of each new morning he feels a traitor
To his plant's good governance. He's jealous,
Too, of her easy growth, her rebellious
Upstarts and volunteers. Oh, he feeds her
Nitrates and water and willingly cedes
Her this place in his living room. No doubt
His care matters; but he knows the mortar
That holds his bones together, what he bleeds,
Means less to her than light, knows the slow rout
Of seasons marks their only true border.

THE POET TAKES A GOOD LOOK AT HIMSELF

In the mirror's portrait he sees plated
On his face his mother's stamp. The question
In his eyes tells just how they're related,
And the hurt line of the mouth. She rests on
Such looks like laurels. And from his father
He learned to live by doing what he ought,
Instead of what he wanted. He'd rather
Not remind himself of this net he's caught
In. Genes, veins, sinews, bones shine from the wall
In every glass. And each time he turns right
Off the interstate, heeding some fresh call
Of blood, drawn to the black wrought-iron light
Above their lawn, he doubts they'll ever see
Each word he writes is meant to set him free.

THE CONSULTANT'S ADVICE TO THE CANDIDATE

Listen, kid, there's only one way to lick
The system: lick what it tells you. I've spent
Big bucks proving that, but it's apparent
You don't buy. Look—the Jew says, "If you prick
Me, I bleed." But he'll give you lotsa *schtick*
To prove he don't. Cuz once they get the scent,
You're ground beef. And don't let some pubescent
Chickie pull your string—I don't care what flick
She's starred in. That stuff'll burst your balloon—
Pow!—like that. No, you pose by your mantel
With the family, cuz the only bootie
Gets votes is bronzed baby. No blue lagoon
For you, pal. And wear that J. Crew flannel
Shirt for photo ops. Think polls. Think duty.

PUSILLANIMOUS POEM

"Other people's ideas of us are dependent largely on what they've hoped for."
—F. Scott Fitzgerald

"I don't want to live—I want to love first and live incidentally."
—Zelda Fitzgerald

Zelda and Scott, that self-destructive pair
We still concede the sheen of glamor to
Because of one great novel and the care
Of critics and biographers, went through
Their reckless years with little time to spare
For anyone beyond themselves. It's true
They suffered in the unrelenting glare
Of blazing notoriety, but who
Can say they didn't choose their cross to bear?
If talent and sheer craziness could do
The same for us, whom do you know who'd dare
To join that drug-and-drink-besotted queue
Lined up to take their chance to play the game
Of trading life and self and soul for fame?

THE POET HAS A MIDLIFE CRISIS

He lives now in a condo of gray brick
With a balcony that neighbors a tree.
This shows the consequence of making free
To choose new ways in middle age. Each tick
Of his wound heart reminds him how the wick
Draws light from the candle, how energy
Flares and fades as night outwaits day. No three-
Sided love wears patiently, yet he'll stick
At endings—always has—and take classic
Refuge in sleep from guilt and grief. But white
Noise, like tearing silk, arcs out of his clock
Radio, then a jingle for Vlasic
Pickles; and morning's comedy stirs slight
Hope of change: one more chip off love's old block.

THE POET CALLS IT A DAY

He grumbles at the dying of the light
And squints at the blank page. The transmission
Of his numbers makes no deep impression
On any soul. He yawns, decides he might
As well turn in. His face, more cause for fright
Each day in his mirror, takes confession
But shrives nothing. His sullen obsession
With craft burrows in him like a termite
Nesting in a lean-to. He sings this dirge
To his reflection, then hits the pillow.
Outside, clouds move in the wind, stars gutter
And fade. He sleeps heavy, dreams of the surge
That fills each green fuse; but as the yellow
Dawn wakes him, he cannot help but shudder.

SPOILED BABY

I must have been six when my adenoids
Came out at the Royal Infirmary
In Glasgow. We were living at Farme Cross
Where three roads intersected at the center
Of the world: Farmeloan Road, Dalmarnock Road,
And Cambuslang Road. One led to my school,
One to Glasgow, one to my grandparents' home.
My mother and I had moved there before
The end of World War II to get ready
For my father's discharge from the army.
Mum told me one day our neighbor's window
Had been pierced by shrapnel the night before.
"Are we winning the war?" I asked her once.
"I don't know," she said. But in time we did.

There in Rutherglen, my father's hometown,
We lived two floors above Grandpa Johnston's
Ground-level flat. I didn't know about
This grandfather who lived downstairs until
Some neighbor boys pointed him out to me,
A shuffling old man with a brown cloth cap,
Thick white hair, and a handlebar moustache.
He and my father never spoke a word
To each other in the five years we lived there.
When I knocked on the door of the old man's flat
And introduced myself, he just grunted.
After that I'd say hello when we passed
Each other on the sidewalk, no melting
Hearts, no happy reunion of father,
Son, and grandson. And when the old man died,
Years later, when we were in the U.S.,
With the McCarthy hearings in full throat,
My uncle made a Transatlantic call
To deliver the news, and my father
Refused to share costs of the funeral.

All that was years ahead as in my ward
At the infirmary the nurse told me
Tonsillectomy patients got ice cream,
But adenoids didn't deserve that treat.
I lay in bed thinking about the dog
I'd brought home at my other grandpa's place;
A wirehaired terrier, black and tan coat,
I'd called him Paddy. His rightful owner
Claimed him, but not before the dog hauled me
Down a flight of stairs, later bit my nose.
I missed him anyway.

       And when no one
Came to visit me, I lay in my bed
In the ward unable to stop my tears.
The boy in the next bed knew I was six
And told me I was a just a spoiled baby.

The shame I felt stayed with me long after
The anesthetic dreams of octopi
And the doctor's snipping of my adenoids.
My parents kept smoking and my breathing
Never did improve until middle age.
The kid in the ward was right all along.

BOOKWORM, A FRAGMENT

Bader's Drugstore on Kercheval and Gray,
Where I first saw books by Mickey Spillane
And the nude Marilyn issue of *Play-
Boy*, before puberty drove me insane,
While I still loved the Monteith Library
And the toasted paper smell of old books,
Hugh Lofting, Robert Heinlein, no Harry
Potter for decades yet to come, with nooks
Where I could sit amid the scent of wax
Polish at leather-topped tables, no cares
Except homesickness for Scotland, in *Pax
Libris,* then return to our place upstairs
From the greasy tavern, three books in hand,
A ten-year-old stranger in a strange land.

REVELATION

You never know when revelation will visit.
The short block between our apartment
On the drab corner of Kercheval
And Springle, above the Blue Ribbon
Tavern with its smells of beer and grease,
And Bader's Drugstore past the vacant
Lot at Kercheval and Gray showed me
Something about myself one fall day.
My father had sent me out to buy—
Something—the *Detroit News*, aspirin,
Who knows what?—with a five-dollar bill
Tucked in my pocket. And I dawdled,
Thinking about birthdays. I was ten,
But I thought I couldn't wait to be
Nineteen, which seemed like the perfect age,
Because I knew it meant no more school,
Leaving me free to read any book
I wanted to.
              But when I arrived
On the mosaic tile of Bader's entry,
I paused and checked my pocket,
Then all the others. Empty, of course.
I turned and retraced my steps, lingered
In the vacant lot between Bader's
And home. I spent at least half an hour
Searching amid grass, weeds, and gravel,
Knowing that the money was long lost.
Strangely, I felt a sense of freedom,
Poised between loss and retribution.
I even found myself whistling,
Shifting from one foot to the other,
Realizing that this was somehow
What the future held in store, as time
Would give and take at no one's bidding.
And after a while I turned for home,
Slow-walking toward what might come next.

ALCHEMY: A SESTINA

I only know it's alchemy,
Turning the everyday metal
Of conversation into gold.
Words lilting in numbers refine
What we say, don't they, when the base
Stuff of our thoughts is touched with fire?

Who could have known words might catch fire
Then at the start, when alchemy
Was still in the dark, and the base
Of all things conceived no metal,
Only the painful light like gold
Loosed from the smelter to refine

The dense black center into gold
Shimmering atoms in the first fire
Of creation? And we refine
Language by our own alchemy
Of technique, testing our mettle,
The brain our neural network's base,

Shimmering up out of the base-
Ment where we mine the mind's pure gold.
What are we after, a medal?
No, we're just hoping for the fire,
The pure word-driven alchemy
We all work somehow to refine.

We're all tinkering to refine
Ourselves or our lives from their base
Beginnings by such alchemy,
Not to get rich with the false gold
Of fame by catching its brief fire
In a lead bottle. That metal

Is its own black poison. That metal
Resists all efforts to refine
Its essence, even in the fire
That should melt and consume each base
Desire for reputation's gold.
But we can't escape alchemy:

We plumb our mettle to its base
As we refine our heart's own gold
In the fire of art's alchemy.

THE GREAT REVISER

I'm the Big Lake, *Mishigami*,
The great reviser.
Along the shore each morning
There's a line of waterworn pebbles till Hell won't have them:
Quartz and tiger-striped agate, blue chert pretending to be agate,
Leland blue slag pretending to be blue chert,
But often exposing itself with a hole clear through.
Siderite masquerading as pebble
With lightning patterns of calcite in the cracks,
Petoskey stones with their subtext of fossilized coral cells,
Unakite with its streaks of green and pink,
Horn coral trumpeting at one end but always making its point,
Like a Paleolithic sonnet,
Petrified wood, Charlevoix stone with its little favositoid eyes—
No, wait, I say, I meant it to be honeycomb coral,
Or stink stone, cratered like an asteroid—
Moonstone—well, feldspar—not to be confused with quartz,
A green and bubbly chunk of Frankfurt slag,
Crinoids in necklacefuls of little rings,
And hosts of other fossils only scholars can identify
As I throw them up from my uncatalogued depths,
All along the Third Coast;
Multicolored pebbles—yes, real pebbles—worn to smoothness
By rubbing around in the bottom of my great pocket
Before I reduce them to grains of sand.
And beach glass: the various bottle browns and greens—
Bud, Labatt's, Heineken, Newcastle, Leinenkugel, they're all here—
But I transform their cliché into smooth little opaque jewels.
The frosted white of old gin and vodka bottles—
Boodle's, Bombay, Tanqueray, Beefeater,
Grey Goose, Absolut, and Stoli,
Scotch and bourbon, too,
J & B, Dewar's, Johnnie Walker, and the whole parade of
    single malts.

I sing the seltzer blues, too, Bromo and Alka,
With Milk of Magnesia on the side,
And the rare and delicate amethyst of old Mason jars.
Driftwood, of course, delicate and skeletal
Or thick and sodden,
Moss and weed, drinking straws, the cups they came in,
Condoms, hypodermics, beach toys, dying bees and ladybugs.
And farther out, kayaks, canoes, skiffs, schooners,
Cabin cruisers, fishing boats, freighters, and ferries,
And their leavings, cargoes and crews.
And far beyond the shipping lanes,
Full fathom fifty,
Who knows what's there in my depths
To be revised tomorrow morning?
The long line of the shore, the metrics of the tide,
Alliteration of the waves,
Beauty and dross, connections churning
Out of all I am.
Collective unconscious?
Don't get me started.

PANTOUM: THEN TO NOW

In cryptic images from alchemy
Jung saw a bridge from then to now,
A rainbow span, not the epitome
Of crackpot science and arcane know-how.

Jung saw a bridge from then to now
In damn near every rendering
Of crackpot science and arcane know-how
From art and physics all the way to the I Ching.

In damn near every rendering
Jung saw alchemy's power of transformation
From art and physics all the way to the I Ching;
And in the heat required for sublimation

Jung saw alchemy's power of transformation
In the creative force of love;
And in the heat required for sublimation
Alchemy and art work hand in glove.

In the creative force of love
The every only god makes certain
That alchemy and art work hand in glove
To help reveal what lies beyond the curtain.

The every only god makes certain
Our crackpot fancies and arcane know-how
Can help reveal what lies beyond the curtain
And trace the alchemy of love from then to now.

THE POET CELEBRATES SCOTS' NEW YEAR SEVEN P.M., EST

Each New Year's Eve at seven, long before
That ball of light brings chaos to Times Square
And people for whom auld lang syne's no more
Than nonsense sing and link hands everywhere,
His wife and he sit quietly and think
Of Hogmanay in Scotland, kith and kin,
And parties past, First Footers coming in
For currant bun or shortbread and a drink,
Whisky for men and sherry for the wives.
They toast their absent friends; eat sweetmeats, too:
He sips on malt, though she prefers champagne.
This moment's pause, before their year rings new
At midnight, stirs a song and helps maintain
The ties of auld lang syne that link their lives.

RADIOACTIVE

> Inspired by *Soap and Juice,* mixed media piece by Ray Bacoskie, and "Radioactive," lyrics by Imagine Dragons (Ben McKee, Dan Platzman, Dan Reynolds, Wayne Sermon, Alexander Grant, Josh Mosser, and Ben Linke)
>
> *All systems go, the sun hasn't died*
> *Deep in my bones, straight from inside*

She laughs and sings, "He's 'Radioactive,'"
As if the Dragons had imagined me.
She's hoping my core's become redactive,
Made sound by sounding, seeded, cancer-free.
The sound of laughter's what we need these days
To make sure that my inward juices flow.
Distraction is the soundest way to faze
Ill thoughts and tidings no one wants to know.
Soap and water, pills, to keep at bay
Post-op infection from the robot drill,
To make sure that I'm ready for the fray
With her who keeps me safe by force of will
And sings, "Whoa-oh, he's radioactive.
Whoa-oh-oh-oh, he's radioactive."

PANTOUM: THE DAMNED CAN TELL US

Something is slouching somewhere to be born
As we all sit and watch it move along
While surrogates and pundits peddle scorn
For all distinctions between right and wrong.

As we all sit and watch it move along,
We wish there were a way to make it go
Where blurred distinctions between right and wrong
Don't really matter on his TV show.

We wish there were a way to make it go
Where bad reality programs should stay.
We've heard too often on his TV show
Success depends on doing things his way.

Where bad reality programs should stay
Is somewhere in the rings of Dante's Hell.
Success depends on doing things his way,
And truth and lies will serve equally well.

But somewhere in the rings of Dante's Hell
The damned could tell us what we ought to know:
When truth and lies will serve equally well,
Nothing can save us, whether friend or foe.

The damned can tell us what we ought to know:
That no distinction between right and wrong
Can hope to save us, whether friend or foe,
If we all sit and watch it slouch along.

UNITED STATES OF DISCORD

Lately I've thought about a dooryard
Bereft of lilacs, out of season,
The jailbreak of circus animals,
The slouch of some beast toward somewhere.
Oh, I don't say the world is likely
To end anytime soon. But for some
People life will probably go back
To a state worse than they imagined
When they cast their lot with the soulless,
Meaning those who have no souls to lose,
And those whose souls are goods for sale.
When Gandhi, MLK, and other
Martyrs couldn't halt the bigotry
And greed and thin-skinned narcissism,
Can the women wearing pussy hats
Bring the bastards down? Can the slick crew
Of pinheads and pundits who broadcast
The ping-pong game they call balanced news
Do more than red ants at a picnic—
Annoy the gluttons at their feasting?
These people seem to hate everything
That's not themselves. So we, who once said
"Make love, not war," have to join the fray
And stand together, bald heads shining,
With all our brothers and sisters
In our united states of discord,
Hoping for the best, doing our best
To inch along to grace together.

SOMETHING TO WORK WITH

>After "Accidental Marks #160," pen and ink drawing
>by Michael Dunn

Give him something to work with, a whirlwind,
A whirlpool, a waterspout, and he'll go
To town, dream up houses thrown to and fro,
Blown to flinders, spun up among the finned
And bright-scaled swimmers sucked skyward and pinned
Among the scribbled clouds, or drawn below
Into the weedy depths as if they'd sinned
Against Neptune or some other chunk-chinned
Deity whose stretched cheeks might puff and blow
Everything beyond the riptide. The eye
Of something stays on the sparrow in flight
Or in the nest and will spare or destroy
Indifferently, as any cat will toy
With whatever mouse comes within its sight,
And never let us ask the reason why.

LOSING WHAT SEEMS MOST DEAR

Abandoning false hope brings clarity
To understand, though pain may lie ahead:
Losing what seems most dear can set us free.

To rise again may call for us to flee
When surging blood would have us fight instead;
Abandoning false hope brings clarity.

And when we realize that victory
So often turns the prize from gold to lead,
Losing what seems most dear can set us free.

We know it's all a matter of degree,
Accepting loss with grace and not with dread;
Abandoning false hope brings clarity.

Of course, we needn't hurry to agree,
But spare a thought for our forgotten dead:
Losing what seems most dear can set us free.

Regard this verse as no more than a plea
For sentiments most often left unsaid:
Abandoning false hope brings clarity;
Losing what seems most dear can set us free.

SOONER THAN LATER

Sooner than later he will cease to be,
He knows; the fragile network of his cells
Is closing checkpoints inexorably.
Though he's not quite prepared for tolling bells,

He knows the fragile network of his cells
Will work its algorithm and run down,
Spiraling inward like nautilus shells
To where "end" is no verb, but just a noun.

Will works its algorithm, too, runs down
As day flows inescapably to night,
And "end" signifies nothing but a noun,
When what some call the soul takes its last flight.

As day flows inescapably to night,
His little life will end its petty creep,
And what some call his soul will take its flight
Where atoms recombine but never sleep.

His little life will end its petty creep,
Shuffled and coiled relativistically
Where atoms recombine but never sleep,
The only way the cosmos sets us free.

Shuffled and coiled relativistically,
Sooner than later he will cease to be
The only way the cosmos sets us free:
Closing all checkpoints inexorably.

RAINBOW

>After *End of the Rainbow,* mixed media piece
>by David Kamm

A solitary dirtbird in pajamas,
He sits at his laptop playing solitaire.
She asks him if he plans to take a shower
Or sit in his grubby idleness all day,
Wasting time. The cards dance as he wins a hand,
And he tells her it's a possibility.
"Write me a poem," she says, and he concedes,
To himself at least, that he's been avoiding
The image of cartridge casings filled with crayons
Instead of bullets, loaded for art, lethal
To nothing except his hope to execute
The end of a rainbow where the urge to write
Might overcome the urge to kill. Poetry,
Like the other arts, solves nothing, but it does
Remind us how much we'd rather live than die.
So what now? Another hand of solitaire?
He asks her if she'll join him in the shower.

MEASURING GRACE

> After mixed media piece by David Bernardys

Grace is something you pray for and wait for,
Looking both ways but mostly up, in case
It comes from Heaven, hoping that fate or
Progress on this human sphere may keep pace,
Measuring with what passes for precise
Gradations our stumbling toward peace,
Even though it's more like rolling the dice
When the chances of snake eyes never cease.
And underneath it all the primeval soup
Keeps roiling, and the telomeres click out
Your allotted span of years when the loop
Of pulsing blood must end. But never doubt,
As the mean hours creep in their petty pace,
You pray for what you are: for you are Grace.

HOLES THAT CAN'T BE PATCHED

When hail volleys like bullets against the screens,
Holes that can't be patched
Mean the frames need new mesh.
Larry at the hardware store
Inherits the town's
Holes that can't be patched.
Do it myself?
With thumbs for fingers,
I could never handle
Holes that can't be patched.
And out of my privilege
I think of other climes,
Of desert places
Where holes are seldom patched
When, against the screens, bullets volley like hail.

SPARROWS

I.

Sparrows
like feathered mice
mate on our balcony.
She seems detached from the process,
but he
flutters above her tail, engaged
by the imperatives
of their nature
and ours.

II.

Flowers on the patio
Sheltered from the autumn breeze
Sparrows flying to and fro
Flowers on the patio
Won't last long, the sparrows know
Soon November nights will freeze
Flowers on the patio
Sheltered from the autumn breeze

III.

On the balcony
A sparrow, feathers fluffed out,
Ready for winter.
Watching from my warm sofa,
I wish I could say the same.

IV.

In Jamaica, years ago,
A friend asked her waiter,
"What are those little birds
Fluttering on the terrace?"
He said,
"We call them sparrows, ma'am."

ROMEO AND JULIET, FROM THE BALCONY

Couples when new all feel the urge to touch
Each other as they walk from place to place,
Grazing, nudging, fondling, though not too much,
Lest friction lead to a full-on embrace
Before they're ready. But quite soon they'll be,
And then the touching will go on for years,
Or so they hope. For over time they'll see
Their hopes transmuted by their unwept tears.
We watch them walking on a small-town street,
He shuffling well ahead, and she behind
Five steps or so, intent on her own beat,
And no one knows what either has in mind.
We spy them from our balcony above
And thank our stars we're old and still in love.

THE POET CONTEMPLATES A SHRINE

A shrine to her sits on the seven-drawer
Chest in their bedroom in this resort town,
Photos slipped into the twists of metal
Monkeys' tails, her younger selves all looking
At him as he picks socks and underwear
From the drawers below. Before the photos
Lake stones sit, smooth Devonian corals,
Petoskeys, Charlevoix stones, crinoids, chert,
Reminders that their time here is no more
Than a fraction of what's gone before them.
A wallet-size of her at seventeen
Smiles down front, forever beyond his reach,
Although she's showering just steps away.
They met in her fourth decade and his fifth,
And they agree that if that seventeen-
Year-old beauty and he had been lucky
Enough to cross paths back then in their youth,
They'd have been a love story ever since.
He'll never hold that young girl in his arms,
But he still gets to hold her every day;
And they know that whatever the lake leaves
On the shore for them to find, whether it's
Coral, beach glass, or pebbles, he and she
Will search together, when at last they go.

DEBORAH, ALWAYS

Always Deborah,
Deborah when the day begins,
At the end of day, Deborah,
Deborah when it all began,
Like falling in a river,
Carried in the rush, Deborah.
A friend asked, "Did you ever
Try to swim ashore?"
Our only answer, "Have you ever
Fallen like that, been carried away?"
Love-drunk acrobats,
We found dactylic rhythm
In the moonglow of cheap motels,
Deborah, Deborah, Deborah.
And when I tried to leave,
To opt for what I thought was sanity,
I had to take the train, because I knew
I couldn't drive myself without turning back.
But its dactyls would not stop muttering
Deborah, Deborah, Deborah.
And after a night of lying, denying,
The current now within,
What Plato told me,
What e e cummings certainly told me,
I threw myself into the morning train,
Its shining rails the current sweeping me back
To Deborah,
Deborah, mother and warrior, judge,
Bringer of peace,
Champion of women, Deborah,
Wife and lover, Deborah,
Artist and partner, Deborah,
Deborah, writer of the hard parts,
Tender of heart, quick to weep, Deborah,

Deborah, teacher and counselor,
Folksinger's girlfriend, Deborah,
Beauty and survivor, Deborah,
Grave and frivolous, Deborah,
Irresistible current, Deborah,
Deborah, Deborah, Deborah,
Deborah when it all began
At the end of day, Deborah,
Deborah when the day begins,
Always Deborah.

ACKNOWLEDGMENTS

My heartfelt thanks to my wonderful editor Diane Kistner; to gifted artists Linda Rzoska and Sarah Matyczyn; to distinguished writing colleagues Richard Katrovas, Elizabeth Knapp, Josie Kearns, and Eric Torgersen. And, finally, to my beautiful Debby, the reason for it all.

I'd like to acknowledge the following publications, in which a number of poems in this collection originally appeared, sometimes in a slightly different form: *Tar River Poetry* ("What the Earth Taught Us"); *The Malahat Review* ("Contract Language" and "Canzone: The Tree in Our Bed"); *The Cumberland Poetry Review* ("The Poet Visits Lake Michigan"); *Stone Country* ("Old Debts"); *Passages North* ("Syzygy in Center Field," winner of Third Prize in the 1990 *Passages North* National Poetry Competition); *Embers* ("Reduction," "A Sort of Sestina," and "Spectators As We Are," published to recognize my being a finalist in the 1990 *Embers* National Chapbook Competition); *Outerbridge* ("Sestina: His Own Bright Music (1952)," "Moon Goddess," and "Double Sonnet: Sunday Drive"); *Encore Magazine* ("Double Sonnet: Sunday Drive," "The Poet Has a Midlife Crisis," "The Poet Considers His Plant"); *Phi Kappa Phi Forum* ("What's Underneath," winner of the *PKP* 2009 Summer Poetry Competition, "The Poet Takes a Good Look at Himself," runner-up in the *PKP* 2012 Summer Poetry Competition, and "The Great Reviser," winner of the *PKP* 2016 Spring Poetry Competition); *Peninsula Poets* ("A Shrine," "Radioactive," and "Pantoum: The Damned Can Tell Us"); *The RavensPerch* ("Spoiled Baby," "Alchemy: A Sestina," "Pantoum: Then to Now"). The title poem in this collection, "Pantoum: Where We're Going, Where We've Been," appears on a broadside with visual art by Linda Lee Rzoska, as does "Alchemy: A Sestina"; "Where We're Going" also placed first in the First Annual Science Slam sponsored by Arkansas State University and performed by the Rough Magic Shakespeare Company. "Pusillanimous Poem" (2019) and "Bookworm, A Fragment" (2018) were Laureate's Choice winners in the Great River Shakespeare Festival/Maria W. Faust

Sonnet Contest, and "Bookworm" also appears in *Better Than Starbucks*. "Romeo and Juliet, From the Balcony" appears in *The Orchards Poetry Journal*. "Revelation" appears in *SHIFT: A Publication of MTSU Write*.

A number of the above poems appear in a chapbook—now out of print—titled *What the Earth Taught Us* (March Street Press, 1996). "Syzygy in Center Field" and "Spectators As We Are" also appear in *New Poems from the Third Coast* (Wayne State University Press, 1999). "Spectators As We Are" and "Sonnet for Carol" appear online in the inaugural issue of *The Weathervane: A Journal of Great Lakes Writing*.

Quite a few of the sonnets in this volume appear, sometimes in somewhat different versions, in a chapbook called *Sonnets: Signs and Portents* (Finishing Line Press, 2014). "The Poet Celebrates Scots' New Year, Seven P.M., EST" also appears in *FEAST: Poetry and Recipes for a Full Seating at Dinner* (Black Lawrence Press, 2014). "Radioactive," inspired by *Soap and Juice,* a mixed media piece by Ray Bacoskie, and the rock song "Radioactive," lyrics by Imagine Dragons (Ben McKee, Dan Platzman, Dan Reynolds, Wayne Sermon, Alexander Grant, Josh Mosser, and Ben Linke), was featured in an exhibition of ekphrastic art, *Expressions in Ink,* Water Street Gallery, Douglas, MI, July 2015. "Something to Work With" and "Sooner Than Later" appear in the Winter 2017 issue of *Third Wednesday,* and "Something to Work With" was included in an exhibition of Michael Dunn's "Accidental Marks" at the Kalamazoo Book Arts Center. Mad Queen Records included my readings of two poems ("These Lovers" and "Contract Language") on an album entitled *The Fear of Drowning: a recorded compilation of Michigan Poets* (Farmington, MI: 1986); and the Arts Council of Greater Kalamazoo included "What's Underneath: After untitled twig-and-fired-ceramic piece by Maria Scott" as part of an Artists and Writers Group Show—work by thirteen visual artists and responses to those works by thirteen writers—at The Epic Center in Kalamazoo, MI.

ABOUT FUTURECYCLE PRESS

FutureCycle Press is dedicated to publishing lasting English-language poetry books, chapbooks, and anthologies in both print-on-demand and Kindle ebook formats. Founded in 2007 by longtime independent editor/publishers and partners Diane Kistner and Robert S. King, the press incorporated as a nonprofit in 2012. A number of our editors are distinguished poets and writers in their own right, and we have been actively involved in the small press movement going back to the early seventies.

The FutureCycle Poetry Book Prize and honorarium is awarded annually for the best full-length volume of poetry we publish in a calendar year. Introduced in 2013, our Good Works projects are anthologies devoted to issues of universal significance, with all proceeds donated to a related worthy cause. Our Selected Poems series highlights contemporary poets with a substantial body of work to their credit; with this series we strive to resurrect work that has had limited distribution and is now out of print.

We are dedicated to giving all of the authors we publish the care their work deserves, making our catalog of titles the most diverse and distinguished it can be, and paying forward any earnings to fund more great books.

We've learned a few things about independent publishing over the years. We've also evolved a unique, resilient publishing model that allows us to focus mainly on vetting and preserving for posterity poetry collections of exceptional quality without becoming overwhelmed with bookkeeping and mailing, fundraising activities, or taxing editorial and production "bubbles." To find out more about what we are doing, come see us at www.futurecycle.org.

THE FUTURECYCLE POETRY BOOK PRIZE

All full-length volumes of poetry published by FutureCycle Press in a given calendar year are considered for the annual FutureCycle Poetry Book Prize. This allows us to consider each submission on its own merits, outside of the context of a contest. Too, the judges see the finished book, which will have benefitted from the beautiful book design and strong editorial gloss we are famous for.

The book ranked the best in judging is announced as the prize-winner in the subsequent year. There is no fixed monetary award; instead, the winning poet receives an honorarium of 20% of the total net royalties from all poetry books and chapbooks the press sold online in the year the winning book was published. The winner is also accorded the honor of being on the panel of judges for the next year's competition; all judges receive copies of all contending books to keep for their personal library.

Made in the USA
Monee, IL
20 March 2020